0

1

?

0

/

D1336780

BRITAIN
SINCE 1948

Technology

Neil Champion

WAYLAND

First published in 2008 by Wayland

Copyright © Wayland 2008

Wayland
338 Euston Road
London NW1 3BH

Wayland Australia
Level 17/207 Kent Street
Sydney, NSW 2000

Editor: Katie Powell
Designer: Phipps Design

British Library Cataloguing in Publication Data

Champion, Neil
Technology. - (Britain since 1948)
1. Technology - Social aspects - Great Britain - History - 20th century -
Juvenile literature
2. Social change - Great Britain - History - 20th century - Juvenile literature
3. Great Britain - Social conditions - 20th century - Juvenile literature
I. Title
303.4'83'0941'09045

ISBN: 978 0 7502 5374 1

Printed in China

Wayland is a division of Hachette Children's Books, an Hachette Livre UK
company.

Picture acknowledgements: Advertising Archives: 8, AP/Topham: 4, Richard
Baker/Corbis: 7, John Bignell/Rex Features: 13, A Barrington Brown/SPL: 24,
Anthony Brown/Istockphoto: front cover r, 27, Digital Vision/Getty Images: 21,
Paul Glendell/Alamy: 15, Hulton-Deutsch/Corbis: 18, Keystone/Topham: 11,
Museum of London/HIP/Topfoto: front cover l, 23, NASA: 28, PA
Photos/Topfoto: 17, Picturepoint/Topfoto: 20, 26, Print Collector/HIP/Topfoto:
22, Charles O'Rear/Corbis: 25, Topfoto: 5, 6, 10, 14, Wayland: 9, 16, 19, 29.

Every effort has been made to clear copyright. Should there be any
inadvertent omission please apply to the publisher for rectification.

Contents

Words in **bold** can be found in the glossary.

Britain in 1948

Life in Britain in 1948 was very different from life today. The population was much smaller – around 47 million then as opposed to over 60 million today. Most people had far fewer possessions, travelled far less, and had a less varied diet.

Another World

Not only did people have a less varied diet but they also looked subtly different – on average Britons were slightly smaller in height and weighed less. Most of the nation's power came from coal. There were no nuclear power stations. About a quarter of all homes did not have electricity. Only one person in 3,000 had a television and hardly any homes had a telephone. There were no computers.

Instead, most people listened to the radio and read newspapers – these were the main forms of entertainment and an important source of news.

The average working person earned about £325 a year. This meant there was little extra money to buy luxury goods. There were also fewer to purchase in the shops and markets. More people lived in the country whereas today most people live in towns and cities.

▲
Family life in the 1940s • *A family in the late 1940s gathering around to watch the new technological wonder, a black and white television showing BBC programmes.*

TIMELINE

1948

Railways are **nationalised**

Start of a golden age of cinema-going

The ship, the *Empire Windrush*, arrives in Britain from Jamaica

The National Health Service is formed

There are 14,500 TV sets in Britain

INVESTIGATE

Rationing food

Most important every day food items were rationed in Britain from the early years of the Second World War until the early 1950s. This meant that people had to queue up with their rationing book to get the small weekly allowance of each item. Here are some of those foods:

- Chocolate
- Tea
- Cheese
- Meat
- Bread
- Sugar
- Bacon
- Butter

▶ **Can you find out what other items were rationed during and after the war?**

▲

The ordinary kitchen · *This photograph was taken in London in the 1950s. It shows a husband and wife in their kitchen doing the washing-up. Technology has very little influence – there is no washing machine, dishwasher, fridge or microwave.*

Emerging from War

In 1948, Britain was emerging from the horrors of the Second World War. This global conflict had lasted from 1939 until 1945. The British **economy** was weak after the end of the war and **manufacturing** was yet to pick up. **Rationing** was in place in 1948 as food, fuel and energy were still in short supply. This was '**Austerity Britain**'.

A Brighter Outlook

Today we have many material possessions – these are the things around us that make our lives easier and more comfortable. In the home we have washing machines, dishwashers, fridges, central heating, non-stick pans, computers and access to the internet. We have cars and cheap air flights, mobile phones and computer-designed tennis racquets made out of special materials such as **carbon fibre**. Most of these things didn't exist in 1948, and those that did were not available to most people. For example, a car was far beyond the financial means of most people, costing well over the average annual salary.

Technology and Society

The advances in technology have had a huge impact on life since 1948. Science and engineering advances in particular have transformed our world. How we make things, the materials that we use, and the cost of producing goods have all been affected.

Technology and Change

These advances have created jobs and wealth for the country and the people living in it, as well as all sorts of goods for us to buy with this increased income, at prices that more and more people have been able to afford. For example, how to manufacture plastic was discovered in 1905. Since 1948, many things once made of wood, metal and cotton could now be made with this new, lighter, cheaper and more versatile man-made material. Plastic could be produced in factories on a large scale, keeping costs down.

INVESTIGATE

Income increases from 1948–2007

Average income per year (in £s)	
1948	325.00
1951	430.00
1961	800.00
1966	1,055.00
1971	1,600.00
2007	31,000.00

Source: British Social Trends since 1990

Why have people's wages risen so dramatically since 1948?

TIMELINE

1948	Britain hosts the summer Olympic Games in London
1951	The Festival of Britain
1953	Coronation of Queen Elizabeth II
1954	Post war rationing ends
1956	Britain opens its first nuclear power station
1960	Britain seeks entry into the European Economic Community (EEC)
1970	Power cuts due to industrial strikes
1989	The World Wide Web is invented

▲ **The motorway** • The London to Birmingham M1 motorway was officially opened on 2nd November, 1959. It signalled the arrival of the motor car into the lives of an increasingly well-off population.

▲
Work and technology • *A modern office, dominated by the technology of information and communications – the computer.*

Greater Opportunities

With the Second World War behind them, people in 1948 could apply themselves to finding many more uses for this new man-made material – plastic. As technological advances were made in other industries, so the use of plastic was extended and developed. Computers started to be made from 1948 onwards. Parts of telephones and televisions were also made using forms of plastic.

SOUNDBITES

In 1964, there was a general election. The Labour leader, Harold Wilson, used the phrase 'the white heat of technological revolution'. When he became Prime Minister he created the Ministry of Technology.

Technology has not only meant a growth in material possessions with the rise in the use of man-made materials. It has also created far greater opportunities to travel since 1948. Not just within the UK but throughout the rest of the world. This has been made possible by new and improved means of transport – the car, plane, ship or train. We communicate far more and far faster than was ever possible in 1948, whether by mobile phone or email.

Technology and Consumerism

The word consumerism refers to people buying goods on a very large scale. This means that the whole society's economy is arranged around producing and consuming these goods.

What Kinds of Goods?

Goods can mean food, clothes, things for the home, cars, sports items, music and jewellery, for example. Some of these are basic needs such as things to eat or clothes to keep us warm. However, in a **consumer society**, even basic things are available in such quantity and variety that people tend to buy far more than they need.

The twin-tub • An advertisement from 1962 selling the latest 'white goods' to the housewife – a twin-tub washing machine. The quotation highlights the defined role of women of the period.

Part of the history of Britain can be seen as society becoming an increasingly consumer society. This has come about through a gradual rise in people's wages and an increase in the availability of manufactured goods at affordable prices. Today, the choice of what we buy and where we choose to buy our goods from is very different from 1948.

TIMELINE

1950	The supermarket, Sainsbury's, opens its first self-service store
1955	ITV and commercial television is launched, starting a new era of advertising
1959	Conservative leader Harold Macmillan tells the country, 'Most of our people have never had it so good'
1968	Tesco opens its first superstore for 'one-stop' shopping
1970	Almost two thirds of homes in Britain have a washing machine
1974	The first video game console goes on sale
1982	Over half of all homes have a telephone
1983	Compact Discs (CDs) are available for the first time
1999	Online shopping is launched by Marks & Spencer
2006	Tesco takes over 30% of all grocery sales in the UK

The Role of Technology

Technology has been changing people's lives in many ways ever since the invention of the wheel thousands of years ago. The **Industrial Revolution** sped up this process in Britain in the late eighteenth century. By the mid twentieth century, Britain was to undergo huge technological change.

Rapid Change

Every aspect of our lives was to be touched by changes in technology: homes, work places, methods of transport, communications, health and leisure were all to be transformed within a few decades. In the 1950s, for example, there were only a few million licensed vehicles on the roads of Britain. This number had increased to just under 20 million by 1981. By 2005, it had risen to 33 million – and those vehicles were being driven almost 500 billion kilometres; eight times further than in 1952. But cars have come at a price, releasing pollution into the atmosphere.

CHANGING TIMES

In 1961, one of the most successful British cars – the Morris Minor – reached 1 million sales. When it first went on sale in 1948, it cost £358, 10s and 7d – more than the average annual salary of £325. Today about a third of all households own two or more cars.

▲ **Consumerism at its height** · Outside a large shopping centre in Britain. Many things can be bought under one roof, ideal for the busy consumer and for fuelling our consumer society.

Technology in the Home

Life in our homes has changed considerably in the years and decades since 1948. Housework is one of the main areas of change. It has become significantly easier with the development of time-saving devices to help with the daily chores.

Doing the Housework

In 1948, housework was a full-time occupation and was hard work. For example, most people had to wash all their clothes by hand and dry them using a combination of a **mangle** and a washing line. The electric washing machine had been invented in America and produced since the early twentieth century. The first automatic washing machine was made by Bendix in 1937.

SOUNDBITES

During the Second World War, women filled the jobs that men had previously done. With the rise of electrical appliances making household chores easier, some women chose to carry on working after the war. As a result attitudes towards women also changed, and so technology indirectly helped to change the role of women.

▲
The mangle • Washing day for a housewife in 1952. Here she is using a mangle to wring out most of the water from the clothes, before she hangs them up to finish off drying.

But in 1948, electric power was absent from a quarter of all UK homes. Even for those who had it, most did not have the money to buy a washing machine.

A Time of Change

The 1950s saw all this change. With rising wages and mass production of washing machines bringing the prices down, more people could afford this labour-saving device. The situation was similar with the dishwasher. A mechanical version had been built and used in America in the late nineteenth century. The commercial world took them up – for example, they were used in restaurants and hotels. However, they did not become common features of homes in Britain until the 1970s. This was the pattern for most home inventions. They existed long before they became available and affordable for the average household.

INVESTIGATE | The dates and inventors of some domestic appliances

Sewing machine	America	Elias Howe	1846
The can opener	America	Ezra Warner	1858
Vacuum cleaner	America	Daniel Hess	1860
Carpet sweeper	America	Melville Bissell	1876
Refrigerator	Germany	Carl von Linde	1876
Telephone	UK	Alexander Graham Bell	1876
Light bulb	America	Thomas Alva Edison	1879
Electric toaster	America	Charles Strite	1919
Microwave oven	America	Percy Spencer	1945

Source: www.inventors.about.com

▶ **Can you find out who invented the first electric kettle?**

Safety • *A modern factory producing washing machines for a major brand name. Here the goods are being inspected before being transported to a warehouse ready for sale.* ▶

Technology and Entertainment

The radio was the main form of entertainment in the home in 1948. The television had been invented in the 1920s and was commercially available by the 1930s but few could afford it. John Logie Baird had made a technological breakthrough and transmitted televised images to a stunned audience in London in 1925. He could not have known that his invention would be one of the most important of the twentieth century.

Voices from history

'Queen Elizabeth II has been crowned at a coronation ceremony in Westminster Abbey in London...An estimated three million people lined the streets of London to catch a glimpse of the new monarch...The ceremony was watched by millions more around the world as the BBC set up their biggest ever outside broadcast to provide live coverage of the event on radio and television. Street parties were held throughout the UK as people crowded round television sets to watch the ceremony.'

The BBC reporting on the Queen's coronation in 1953.

Entertainment in the Home

In 1936, it is estimated that there were approximately 100 TV sets in the country. The British Broadcasting Corporation (BBC) was the only channel in 1936 and transmitted the coronation of King George VI in that same year. The picture was poor by modern standards and the signal was easily broken. However, this was the beginning of one of the most influential inventions of the twentieth century. In the following year, popular sporting events were televised – the Oxford and Cambridge boat race, Wimbledon, the FA Cup final and Test match cricket.

Audiences were becoming hooked. Thousands of people were to join what was a revolution in telecommunications by buying a TV set over the coming decades. By 1948, there were 14,500 TV sets in the country. Colour came to our televisions in 1967 and by the 1970s, almost all homes in Britain had a television.

Going to the Cinema

Film-going became one of the most popular forms of entertainment in the early twentieth century before television really took hold in people's homes. In the late 1940s, Ealing Studios in London produced a series of great films for the cinema-goers, such as *Passport to Pimlico* and *Kind Hearts and Coronets*.

This was the golden age of the cinema when 30% of the population went to see a film at least once a week. With falling audience numbers and closing cinemas, technology was used to try to reverse the trend. Wider screens (called Cinemascope) and 3-dimensional films were introduced in the 1950s. Special effects and animation replaced these in the 1980s and 1990s, with increasingly sophisticated technology. Today, computer animation and computer generated imagery enable film-makers to mix real actors with stunning backgrounds and monsters.

Getting Around: The Car

Like the television, the mass production of the motor car was to signal a major change in how we live our lives and what it is possible for us to do.

Mass Production of the Motor car

In the first half of the twentieth century technological advances in the manufacture of the **internal combustion engine** allowed the car to become smaller, more reliable and cheaper. Most importantly of all, it could be produced in huge numbers due to the use of assembly line construction. America led the way, with the Model T Ford. The Morris Minor became the car that was to put Britain on wheels, becoming the country's first affordable car. Along with the development of car technology came a road-building programme.

The Road Network

Today, there are over 380,000 kilometres of road network throughout Britain. The network copes with well over 30 million licensed vehicles, about four times the number of vehicles compared with the early 1960s. This staggering growth in vehicle transport indicates that most families now have at least one car. It also reflects the fact that most of the things we buy today have been transported by road at some point, taken to a warehouse and moved on again to the shops.

▲

Testing times • In 1960, a Ministry of Transport test (called the MOT) was brought in for all cars over 10 years old. They had to be examined every year for safety and roadworthiness.

TIMELINE

1948	380,000 kilometres of trunk road network in the UK
1958	The M6 Preston bypass is opened
1959	The 'Mini' is manufactured and goes on sale for £496
	The M1 motorway is opened
	Car seat belts are introduced
1986	The M25 motorway is opened

Energy • *This man is filling his car with bio-diesel made from used cooking oil. In our world today, with its problems of global warming and threats to oil supplies, there are scientists and engineers searching for alternative energy sources such as this.*

CHANGING TIMES

Hybrid vehicles that use two or more sources of fuel are becoming more common. In 2000, fewer than 10,000 were sold in the UK. In 2006, nearly 100,000 were sold.

The Engine and the Fuel

The success of the car is down to its internal combustion engine and its fuel (either petrol or diesel). The process of refining oil was discovered in the mid nineteenth century, but up until the 1950s coal remained the most important source of energy in the world.

As the car became increasingly important, so did oil. Petrol and diesel both come from crude oil, which is found in many countries and is widely available. The development of the engine goes hand in hand with the rise of this energy source. Today, alternative fuels are being sought as oil is not a **renewable source** and will run out.

Getting Around: The Train

Railways have been an important form of transport in Britain since the second half of the nineteenth century. Since the invention of the **steam locomotive** in 1825 and the development of the rail network, people and goods have been moved from place to place by train. Trains largely replaced the horse and carriage for long distance travel.

Decline and Nationalisation

By 1948, the railway was in decline due to a lack of money to improve services. The new Labour government that had taken over in 1945 had nationalised the entire network. This included the underground rail service in London. A new age of the train was ushered in. In 1948, many trains in use still ran on steam – a technology that had been in service for over 140 years. The new British Transport Commission (BTC) brought in a mix of diesel and electric driven trains to modernise the entire network, but steam engines were not totally replaced until the 1960s.

The steam train • *A steam train in the 1960s on the Liverpool to Carlisle line, one of the last commercial steam trains to run. Since the late 1940s, steam was replaced with electric and diesel engines.*

TIMELINE

1955	1,000 miles of electrified track in Britain
1967	The last passenger steam train on a main line is taken out of service
1975	601 million passenger journeys are taken on the London Underground
1988	Clapham Junction rush-hour train crash kills 35 people
2002	Potters Bar rail crash kills seven people and injures 70 people
2003	An estimated 1 billion passenger journeys are made on trains in Britain

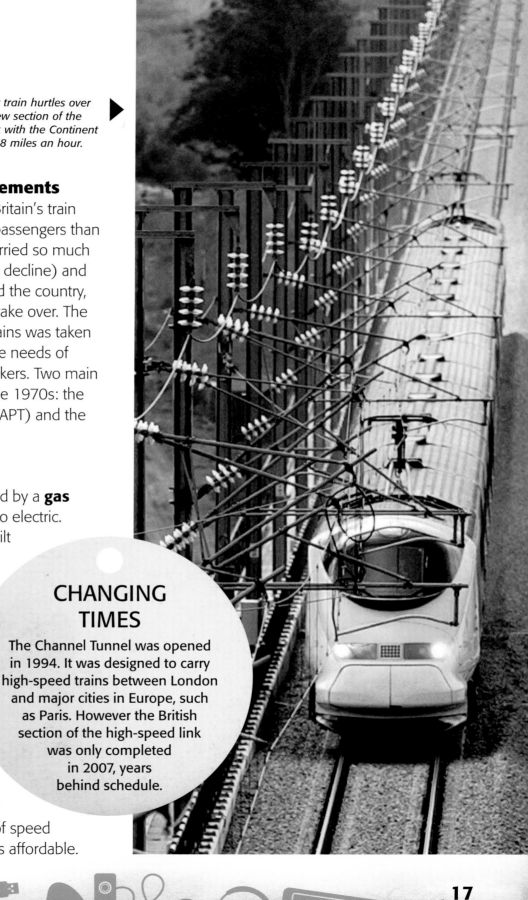

The fast way to travel • *A Eurostar train hurtles over the Medway Bridge in Kent on a new section of the high-speed Channel Tunnel rail link with the Continent in 2004. It can reach a speed of 208 miles an hour.*

Technological Improvements

By the 1950s and 1960s, Britain's train service was carrying more passengers than **freight**. Trains no longer carried so much coal (as this industry was in decline) and other types of goods around the country, as road transport began to take over. The quest for faster and safer trains was taken up by engineers to serve the needs of commuters and holiday makers. Two main types of train emerged in the 1970s: the Advanced Passenger Train (APT) and the High Speed Train (HST).

Speed and Safety

The APT was at first powered by a **gas turbine** but later changed to electric. Its secret was that it would tilt around bends enabling it to keep up its speed – up to 155 miles per hour when using old track. However, it was scrapped in 1984 as the technology was not thought to be safe enough at high speed. The HST won the battle, although it did not tilt and could only reach 125 miles per hour. It provided the right balance of speed and safety, at a cost that was affordable.

CHANGING TIMES

The Channel Tunnel was opened in 1994. It was designed to carry high-speed trains between London and major cities in Europe, such as Paris. However the British section of the high-speed link was only completed in 2007, years behind schedule.

Getting Around: Boats and Planes

Britain has been a **maritime** nation for many years. Its ships have sailed the oceans, taking British manufactured goods to other countries and bringing back raw materials (such as cotton) and exotic food (such as spices and sugar).

Crossing the Channel

In 1900, the Merchant and Royal Navies combined had more vessels than the rest of the world put together. Decline set in with the rise of air travel from the 1950s onwards, and the loss of **colonies** from the **British Empire**.

However, technological advances in certain types of sea travel enabled sea transport to continue operating. These included the hovercraft and high-speed jet foil craft.

▲

Hovercraft • The hovercraft arrives at Dover harbour on the very first Channel crossing from France in 1959.

The English Channel is one of the busiest shipping lanes in the world. Modern vessels take people across it in under an hour, a time that still rivals the Channel Tunnel high-speed train link.

The Rise of Aircraft

The first aircraft with an engine to take to the skies was the *Kitty Hawk*, built by the Wright brothers in 1903. Taking inspiration from the Wright brothers' vision, advances were made to make flights more efficient and safe.

TIMELINE

1955	The hovercraft is invented
1976	Concorde makes its first commercial flight
2004	334 airports in the UK
2005	The largest passenger plane, the *Airbus A380* takes its first flight in April. It can take a maximum of 853 people and has been called the Super Jumbo

Concorde • *The Anglo-French supersonic passenger aircraft, Concorde, takes off on its transatlantic flight from Europe to America.*

SOUNDBITES

The first commercial supersonic passenger plane was Concorde; pioneered in the late 1960s, it made its first passenger flight in 1976. It had a cruising speed of just over 2,000 kilometres per hour. But it stopped flying in 2003 after a fatal air crash in July 2000 brought bad publicity and falling passenger numbers.

The craft themselves became much larger and were able to fly further (*Kitty Hawk* could only fly for 40 metres and be in the air for 12 seconds).

The jet engine was invented in 1929 by an Englishman called Frank Whittle. This was the piece of technology that allowed aircraft to go faster and to carry more people. In the 1950s, air travel was only available to rich or important people. However by the 1960s, there were far more aircraft and the first mass market package holidays became available to destinations such as Spain.

The Computer Industry

It is hard to imagine life without the computer and the benefits of tools such as access to the internet and email. These amazing pieces of technology influence most aspects of our lives today – how we shop, book holidays, do our homework, communicate with our friends, plan our week, bank our money and so on.

The Amazing Microchip

The invention of the **microchip** in 1958 marked a significant change in the computer. It allowed electronic circuits to become very small and much more powerful. Microchips could also be mass-produced very cheaply.

The computer in 1948 • *An IBM (International Business Machines) computer in 1948. It fills the whole room.*

The Rise of the Computer

Although the computer had been invented by 1948, the important part it would eventually play in our lives was not then known. A computer in 1948 was huge, yet it could do only a fraction of the tasks a laptop computer can do today. By the 1960s, there were not many around – perhaps only 20,000 worldwide. Each cost about £70,000 for something we would pay a few hundred pounds for today.

TIMELINE

1948	The first computer is used
1964	The computer mouse is invented
1971	IBM invents the floppy disk
1981	Microsoft develop MS-DOS operating system
1985	*Microsoft Windows* is launched
1989	The World Wide Web is invented by Tim Berners-Lee

Advances today • *Today, computers are much smaller and lighter than they were in 1948. This allows some computers (laptops) to be transported from room to room and can even be used outside, for example on train journeys.*

This in turn paved the way for the modern computer, as well as technology such as the mobile phone and all other digital electronic equipment. This technology allowed the world to communicate faster, more cheaply and more frequently than had ever been possible. Music, images, videos and animations could all now be moved around electronically and downloaded to any personal computer.

CHANGING TIMES

In 2007, the world's fastest and most powerful computer was the IBM Blue Gene/L. It could do over 280 trillion calculations a second and had a 32,768 GB main memory. It ran on PowerPC 440 700MHz processors.

Entering our Homes

For years computers were used only by businesses, the military and in space programmes. It was to be quite a while before they became common features of our homes. Cost was one reason. Another reason was the time it took engineers to reduce the size of the average computer and make it useable by people with no training in computer languages. One landmark in the journey to making the computer was the invention of the mouse in 1964. This made moving the cursor on the screen much easier. Another landmark was the birth of the computer software company, Microsoft. This company did more than any other to make using the computer easy and accessible for most people through the development of its *Windows* software, which was launched in 1985.

Communications

As with the computer industry, the world of communications has changed from that which our parents or grandparents would have recognised. For example, today we send over 1 billion text messages a week. The very first text message was sent in 1989 and by the 1990s, texting was becoming increasingly common.

From Telegrams to Satellite Phones

Gone are the hand-delivered **telegrams** that brought important news in the 1940s and 1950s – stopped by British Telecom in 1996 due to competition from email and mobile phones. The last horse-drawn mail van was taken out of service in London in 1949. We still have a postal service and communicate by letter today.

TIMELINE

1956	The first transatlantic telephone cable is laid
1965	The Post Office Tower is opened in London
1969	The internet is conceived
1989	The World Wide Web is invented
2002	An estimated 50 million mobile phones in use in the UK
	An estimated 35 million domestic land lines in use in the UK

▲

The SS Great Eastern • *The SS Great Eastern in 1865, an iron-made steam ship built in the UK, is shown here laying a telegraph cable that will go underneath the Atlantic Ocean from Britain to America.*

However, we write far fewer letters than we did between the 1950s and the 1980s. We still have payphones in the street, but there is no need for an operator at an exchange to put us through when we make an international call. We are able to communicate more easily using a range of different devices.

For example, expeditions going to Everest or Antarctica can keep in contact with their families by using phones with a satellite link-up. This combines the technology of space with that of communication tools.

Electronic Mail

The telephone has been with us for many decades, although in the late 1940s and through the 1950s very few people actually owned one. Today, we have land lines and mobile phones. One major form of communication we have today that we did not have even in the 1980s, is email. This means of sending messages and attachments via the internet from one computer to another has changed the way personal and business communications take place. Most homes and businesses in Britain today have a computer that is hooked up to the internet. This makes communication by email very easy and therefore popular.

An early telephone exchange • *These women worked at a telephone exchange in London. The photograph was taken in 1951 and it shows how the operators put calls through from one telephone to another using a switchboard. This is all automated today.*

Technology and our Health

The National Health Service (NHS) was set up in 1948 and is still with us today, but much has changed in its procedures and capabilities. Scientific and technological advances made in medicine and hospital equipment since the middle of the twentieth century have considerably extended the life span of the average person in Britain.

Our average time spent recovering from operations is far lower as well. Anaesthetics, X-rays (discovered in 1895), ultrasounds and organ transplants (from the 1960s onwards) have all contributed to our longer lives. So, too, have the discovery and use of medicines such as antibiotics, discovered in 1928.

Living Longer

At the beginning of the twentieth century the average **life expectancy** at birth in the UK was 47 years. By the end of the century it was 77 years. Advances in medicine and technology have also made types of surgery possible that would have been impossible 60 years ago.

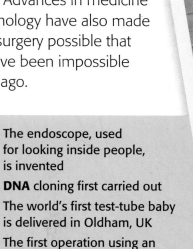

TIMELINE

1956	The endoscope, used for looking inside people, is invented
1973	**DNA** cloning first carried out
1978	The world's first test-tube baby is delivered in Oldham, UK
1982	The first operation using an artificial heart is carried out in America
1987	The first laser operation on a patient's eye
2003	The human genome is decoded

Watson and Crick • *James Watson and Francis Crick in 1953 demonstrate the structure of the DNA molecule that they had recently discovered. This discovery unlocked the door for modern gene-based medical therapies.*

'The first heart and lung transplant operation to be performed in Britain was successfully carried out today. Swedish journalist, Lars Ljungberg, underwent the transplant, receiving the organs of a woman from the south of England who died yesterday. It took a team of 20 doctors and nurses at the specialist heart unit, Harefield Hospital, in north London, more than five hours to carry out the operation. Mr Ljungberg is said to be recovering well from the operation and is recuperating on an isolation ward in the intensive care unit there.'

On the 6th December 1983, the BBC News website reported on a milestone event in British medical history.

Biotechnology and the Future

Since DNA was discovered 50 years ago and the human **genome** was decoded in April 2003, medical technology has moved into a new phase. We now know that our entire body mechanisms are controlled by 30,000–40,000 genes. It is within our grasp to help and maybe even cure diseases that people are born with and types of cancer that have proved most difficult to tackle by using **stem cell technology**.

Laser technology • A delicate operation on a patient's eye using the latest fibre optic and laser technology.

The Science of Materials

Technology has delivered dozens of man-made materials that have taken over from more traditional sources, such as cotton, wool and wood. Today we have lots of different types of plastics; fibres such as polyester, elastaine, and nylon; and materials that will stop a bullet like **Kevlar**.

From the Lab to the High Street

These materials have all come from the laboratory and found their way into every day items such as clothing, computers, mobile phones and cars. They have enabled designers to make lighter, stronger and harder wearing goods. It is not just the item that we have to look at when see how far technology has affected our lives, but also what the item is made out of.

Nylon • This man is working at a factory in Wales making nylon. This artificial material was invented in 1935. Here it is being stretched into long fibres and cooled, and then wound onto cylinders.

Materials go hand in hand with our ability to use technology to make our lives better. For example, without being able to make use of **silicon**, we could not have the microchip. Therefore computers would still be large and slow.

CHANGING TIMES

In the 1950s, people's clothing was made from natural fibres, such as cotton, linen and wool. Today, special waterproof and breathable fabrics that were originally designed by NASA for space flights, are far lighter and more comfortable than waxed cotton materials or heavier nylon outerwear.

TIMELINE

1948	Velcro is invented
1954	The first cooking pan coated with Teflon is produced
1965	Kevlar is invented
1966	Fibre optics are invented
1976	Gore-tex is invented

The silicon chip • *A close-up photograph of a silicon chip. This miniature integrated circuit eventually meant computers could be made smaller and with more power.*

Extreme Environments

Man-made materials have also enabled us to venture into hostile environments. Whether it is the top of Everest, the densest jungle or the deepest ocean; warmer, cooler, lighter and stronger materials play a part in every successful expedition. Using materials that are designed for a specific purpose also helps in each different environment – windproof, waterproof, extremely warm and breathable materials, all these have been developed by scientists in extreme conditions.

INVESTIGATE The uses of new man-made materials since 1948

Gore-tex

This man-made fabric has been around since 1976. It is waterproof but allows moisture from the body to pass through it. The garment stays dry on the inside and the outside. Gortex fabric has millions of tiny holes, each one 20,000 times smaller than a raindrop, but bigger than the moisture droplets from our sweat making the fabric waterproof and breathable.

> **What uses would this material have in our every day clothes?**

Technology in Space

The exploration of space by sending a craft out of Earth's orbit started in October 1957, when the Soviet Union launched *Sputnik 1*, an unmanned satellite. It escaped Earth's atmosphere by means of rocket technology, most of which had come out of the Second World War.

Voices from history

'I went to see the Moon landing live on a massive TV screen in Trafalgar Square – actually it was a huge bank of TV screens all of which showed a little bit of the picture, but altogether formed one picture. It just seemed amazing at the time and perhaps rather unbelievable. We were in a huge crowd of people in the square and could see the Moon in the sky. It was difficult to connect with what we had just seen on TV. It is amazing what technology can do.'

A spectator's feelings at watching the first man on the Moon in 1969.

TIMELINE

1957	The first space flight is made
1961	The first manned space flight takes place
1969	The first Moon landing is made
1977	The *Voyager 1* space probe is launched, orbiting Saturn and Jupiter
1981	The first Space Shuttle is launched
2007	The largest telescope on Earth is built on the Canary Islands at a cost of £100 million

▲
Man on the Moon • *Neil Armstrong sets foot on the surface of the Moon on 20th July, 1969 – the first man ever to do so. He was to spend over two hours there before making the return journey with fellow astronauts, Buzz Aldrin and Michael Collins.*

First in Space

The first human being to enter space was the Russian Yuri Gagarin in April 1961. The 1960s, saw both Soviet and American scientists involved in developing technology to send more spacecrafts into space. Both countries wanted to go into space both for military purposes and to put a man on the Moon. This eventually happened when the American Neil Armstrong set foot on the Moon in July 1969.

Since this early period of space exploration, space agencies have tried to send probes to distant planets. In 1971, the Russians landed a probe on Venus and in 1974 the Americans explored Mercury. In 1990, the *Hubble Space Telescope* was launched and sent back to Earth a new generation of images of deep space millions of light years away.

Satellites

There are now many hundreds of satellites in space orbiting Earth, put there by various nations. Satellite technology has come a long way since the early days of the late 1950s and early 1960s. One of the most interesting things is how flexible their uses are and how they have helped other technologies to develop.

SOUNDBITES

Scientists have been developing technologies to allow us to mine asteroids. Near-Earth asteroids, might be within the range of commercial mining. Inside their rocks they have important elements such as iron and nickel. These raw materials could be processed and sent back to Earth.

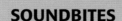

Orbiting Earth • Sputnik 1 *was the first unmanned satellite to be sent into space by the Soviet Union in October 1957. Since then many more have been sent into space for all sorts of reasons such as researching other planets or gathering data about our own planet.*

For example, the military use satellites to spy on other armed forces. They are also used in the communications industry and for navigation. Satellites are used to help forecast the weather on Earth and as an observatory to look outwards into the rest of space and send back images to scientists on Earth.

Timeline
Highlights in the History of Britain since 1948

1948 The first modern computer is used

1948 The railways are nationalised

1951 The Festival of Britain

1952 Elizabeth II becomes Queen

1953 James Watson and Francis Crick publish their discovery of the DNA molecule

1955 ITV commercial television starts

1956 The first transatlantic telephone cable is laid

1956 Britain's first nuclear power station, Calder Hall, is turned on

1957 The first space flight takes place

1957 Britain tests its first hydrogen bomb

1958 The first stretch of motorway is opened in Britain (part of what is today the M6)

1961 The birth of the Campaign for Nuclear Disarmament (CND)

1964 The computer mouse is invented

1969 The internet is conceived

1969 Concorde makes its first flight

1969 Man lands on the Moon and live TV pictures are transmitted back to Earth

1970 Power cuts hit the nation

1973 Britain joins the European Economic Community (EEC)

1975 Prestel launches its first view data system in the UK, linking computer data with the TV screen

1976 Gore-tex is patented in America

1978 The first test-tube baby in the world is born in England

1979 Margaret Thatcher becomes the first female British Prime Minister

1981 Microsoft develop the MS-DOS operating system

1985 *Microsoft Windows* is launched

1989 The World Wide Web is invented by Tim Burners-Lee

1997 The funeral of Princess Diana is watched around the world by 2.5 billion people

1999 Online shopping is launched by Marks & Spencer

2002 An estimated 50 million mobile phones are in use in the UK

2003 The human genome is decoded

2007 The largest telescope on Earth is built on the Canary Islands at a cost of £100 million

Glossary

'Austerity Britain' The period (1945–1951) after the Second World War when rationing of food and clothes meant the population of Britain was under-fed and had to queue for basic items

British Empire The regions of the world (for example India, Australia, New Zealand and Kenya) that were once ruled by Britain

carbon fibre A material made from thin, strong bits of carbon

colonies Countries or areas under the political rule of another country

consumer society A society that buys lots of goods to make its wealth

DNA Deoxyribonucleic acid – the building blocks of life, forming the parts of our body cells that carry the instructions that make us what we are

economy A system in which a country organises the production of goods and services

freight Goods transported by train or other means

gas turbine A type of engine driven by hot, expanding air (which is a gas)

genome All the DNA material of a living organism inherited from parents is known as the genome

Industrial Revolution The period in Britain in the late eighteenth and early nineteenth century in which manufacturing was mechanised to make it faster and more efficient

internal combustion engine An engine in which fuel (petrol or diesel) is ignited inside a cylinder and used to power a machine

Kevlar A man-made fibre invented in the 1960s. It is five times stronger than steel and is used as body armour

life expectancy how long people can expect to live to

mangle A hand-worked machine used to remove water from clothes

manufacturing Producing something on a large scale

maritime A word that relates to the sea and a nation, such as Britain

microchip A tiny integrated circuit

nationalise To take out of private ownership and make the property of the nation as a whole

rationing The process by which food and clothing are made available to people on a limited basis due to shortage or difficulty obtaining them

renewable source A type of energy that can be used again and again for example, wind and water

silicon One of the 94 elements that occur naturally on Earth. It is grey or brown in colour, often forming crystals

steam locomotive A vehicle, such as a train or steam engine, that is driven by using the power of steam

stem cell technology Special cells in our bodies that have the potential to be used to make any new organ

telegram A message sent by telegraph and delivered in written or printed form

FURTHER INFORMATION

📖 Books

Britain Since World War II: Media and Entertainment
Colin Hynson
(Franklin Watts, 2007)

Explore History: Britain Since 1930
Jane Shuter
(Heinemann Library, 2005)

🖱 Websites

http://www.statistics.gov.uk
Discover many different statistics about life in Britain from average house prices in your area to the number of people who are unemployed

http://www.parliament.uk
Find out about Britain's parliament and its plans for the future